"America has opened her heart to me. And I come to you—America—with sentiments of friendship, reverence, and esteem. I come as one who already knows you and loves you, as one who wishes you to fulfill completely your noble destiny of service to the world."

Louis Weber, President
Publications International, Ltd.
3841 West Oakton Street
Skokie, Illinois 60076

Permission is never granted for commercial purposes
Printed in Yugoslavia
j i h g f e d c b a
ISBN 0-517-65108-4

This edition published by
Beekman House
Distributed by Crown Publishers, Inc.
225 Park Avenue South
New York, New York 10003

BEEKMAN HOUSE
New York

TABLE OF CONTENTS

TABLE OF CONTENTS

A dark stocking cap covers the familiar white hair, and sunglasses hide the familiar face, but who else pauses at the top of a slope to lead his skiing party in prayer? Who else but the beloved Polish pope, John Paul II. This complex man loves to sing but does not hesitate to explore the deepest theology. He used to write poetry under a pen name and now writes encyclicals that speak to the world. This man, who once worked in a stone quarry and who volunteered to care for war refugees, challenges dictators and winks at children. This man, who was blacklisted by the Nazis, was at the top of the list when the leaders of the Roman Catholic church sought a new supreme pontiff.

This is a unique man who on October 16, 1978, overturned 455 years of tradition and became the first non-Italian since the Middle Ages to be elected pope. The spiritual leader of 600 million Catholics around the world, John Paul II has a warm, powerful personality. He touched millions during his first visit to the United States in 1979. When he came to the U.S. in September 1987, huge crowds lined the routes of his motorcades just to catch a glimpse of the pope, waited for hours to hear his words, and stood in the rain and hot sun to pray with him.

Who is this man, and what molded his life and character? How did Karol Wojtyla, the schoolboy actor, become Father Wojtyla and then rise up the hierarchical ladder in the church? What compels him to travel throughout the world to spread the word of God?

Pope John Paul II came into the world as the second son of a former school teacher and a recruiter for the Polish military. He was born on May 18, 1920, in Wadowice, a small town in southern Poland, and was baptized Karol Jozef Wojtyla (pronounced "voy-TEA-was") on June 20 of that year.

Little Karol, who was named after his father, received his early education in the parish school. A treasured family photograph shows him in the traditional white suit on the day he made his First Communion. He attended Mass every morning and often stopped to pray on the way home from school.

When Karol was not quite nine, his mother, Emilia, died. She had been in poor health and passed away while delivering a stillborn daughter. Karol and his older brother, Edmund, were raised by their father alone from then on. Wojtyla was a warm-hearted, pious man, who could also be a strict disciplinarian. He not only cooked and kept house, but he also found time to guide Karol's studies and to take a regular evening walk with his younger son during which they often talked about ethics and politics.

Above: Pope John Paul at prayer in the Italian Alps in 1984

Opposite: Karol Wojtyla at 12 years old in 1932

While his brother was in medical school, young Karol worked to help support the family. He found time to play goalie for the local soccer team, and showed off his athletic ability by taking daredevil swims in the flooded Swaka River. He was also president of the school sodality, a student religious organization.

Three years after his mother's death, Karol's brother, an intern who was preparing to become a doctor, contracted scarlet fever from a patient and died in the epidemic of 1932.

Even at an early age, Karol enjoyed speaking before crowds. He did expert impersonations of his teachers, and his natural showmanship led him to discover the stage. He won roles in several school productions and in 1937, starred in and helped to direct a drama club production that toured several towns in the region.

When he was 17, Karol Wojtyla passed his high school exams and was accepted at the Jagiellonian University in Krakow. His father, who had retired from the military, moved to Krakow and took an apartment so Karol could continue his education.

At this point in his life, the man who would become pope was not even sure he wanted to be a priest. But in Krakow, Wojtyla became friends with Jan Tyranowski, whom he credits with cultivating his interests in philosophy, meditation, prayer, and Christian mysticism. Tyranowski, an uneducated but deeply religious man, brought Karol into a "living rosary" prayer group. But even though Karol was enrolled in the philosophy department at the university, he spent his free time with an experimental troupe known as the Rhapsodic Theater. He wanted to study literature and become an actor. But all that was to change. A turning point came on September 1, 1939. Karol Wojtyla was serving as an altar boy at Mass in Krakow when the German bombs began to fall on Poland.

The Nazi occupation forced both the university and the theater group to go underground. In order not to be deported or imprisoned, Wojtyla took a job as a stonecutter. The work was hard, and

Above: Emilia Wojtyla, Karol's mother, with his older brother, Edmund,

in a photograph that was probably taken a few years before Karol was born

at night he took classes, studied, wrote poetry, and rehearsed plays. But the regular quarry workers were sympathetic toward the students, and Karol was given a place on the crew that placed explosives in the rock, a dangerous but less physically demanding job than cutting stone. Two years later he found work in a chemical plant, unloading lime and stoking boilers. Even then he showed himself to be a leader; he lobbied for improved working conditions and persuaded management to open a recreation center for his fellow workers.

Throughout the occupation, Karol secretly continued his education and his acting career. Performing plays and reading poems helped to keep alive the suppressed Polish culture, but Wojtyla was doing much more for the resistance. He was active in an underground Christian democratic organization, and Jewish authorities have testified that he helped Jews find refuge from the Nazis. These kinds of activities for the resistance put the future pope on the German blacklist and forced him to disappear suddenly from his job at the chemical plant in 1944. But by that time the young man had already made an important career decision.

Karol's beloved father died in 1941, and later that year while he was laid up from a streetcar accident, Wojtyla gave serious thought to the religious life. He considered becoming a Carmelite brother. But at that point in his life, he was not ready to give up his ambition to become a great actor. Soon after he was released from the hospital, however, he was sideswiped by a German army truck and again found himself hospitalized. This second convalescent period gave him time to reconsider his priestly vocation. By 1942, he was studying for the priesthood.

Wojtyla and other seminarians feared reprisal from the Nazis and took refuge in the residence of the archbishop of Krakow during the last year of the war. Cardinal Adam Stefan Sapieha hid him and 19 other students while they attended secret theology classes. Once the war was over, Karol Wojtyla began to study for his life's work in a more conventional way.

Above: Ever since he was a schoolboy, Pope John Paul has been at ease on stage.

Vast crowds cheered the pope, wearing a sombrero, in Oaxaca, Mexico, in 1979.

Karol Wojtyla's exceptional intellectual gifts were apparent to his superiors when the young priest was ordained November 1, 1946. The prince-archbishop of Krakow, Cardinal Sapieha, sent the new priest to Rome to continue his studies, an honor that is reserved for those young priests whose qualities make them stand out among their peers.

The 26-year-old Polish priest was assigned to the Angelicum University in Rome. He graduated

as a doctor of divinity, magna cum laude, in 1948, writing his dissertation on "Problems of Faith in the Works of St. John of the Cross." During his two years in Rome, Father Wojtyla lived in the Belgian College and spent his vacations in Belgium and France where he ministered to Polish workers and other refugees displaced by the war.

When he returned to Poland in 1948, Father Wojtyla became a pastor at St. Florian Church in Krakow. He took a doctorate in theology at the Jagiellonian University and served as the students' chaplain and counselor before the Communist government abolished the religion department at the university.

Father Wojtyla then became a professor of moral theology at the major seminary in Krakow, and in 1954, he began to teach ethics at the Catholic University of Lublin in Poland, the only university in Eastern Europe that was not run by the government.

Father Wojtyla was on a summer camping trip in 1958 when he was called back to Krakow because Pope Pius XII had appointed him auxiliary bishop. He was only 38 years old, and the appointment took many by surprise. His rise through the church hierarchy had begun.

By 1962, Bishop Wojtyla was in effect the head of the diocese. He had been named vicar general of Krakow in 1961, and when Archbishop Baziak died the following year Bishop Wojtyla took over his duties. Pope Paul VI made him the archbishop of Krakow on January 13, 1964.

Above: Father Wojtyla in 1946

These were important times for the Catholic church. Pope John XXIII had called for an ecumenical council, throwing open the windows and letting in "fresh air," as he called it.

Archbishop Wojtyla was present for every session of the Second Vatican Council. He became an influential council member, writing important documents and bringing his theological expertise into the discussions. He called his personal experience with Communism to the attention of the council and was particularly forceful in encouraging the leaders of the Catholic church to increase their efforts to secure religious liberty throughout the world.

Archbishop Wojtyla continued to face a hostile government when he returned to Poland after the Vatican Council. He criticized the government repeatedly for its violations of the human rights of the Polish people. For 20 years, he fought to get a church built in Nowa Huta, a post-war "new town" that had no church. Eventually, that church was built.

Even though religious education was officially restricted in Poland, Archbishop Wojtyla put into action the decrees of Vatican II. Adult religious study groups were formed in the parishes and family ministries were promoted, as were ministries for the sick and the disabled. The teachings of the council fathers at Vatican II were brought directly to the people.

Archbishop Wojtyla often used the power of the faith of the Polish people to win concessions from the Communists. In 1967, Pope Paul VI recognized his achievements by raising him to the rank of cardinal, and in 1976, he asked the cardinal to conduct a retreat for him and the rest of the papal household.

When a heart attack took the life of Pope John Paul I after he had reigned for only 34 days, the sacred college of cardinals assembled at the Vatican for the second time in two months to pick a new pope. The man they chose on October 16, 1978, was the would-be actor, Cardinal Karol Wojtyla.

Above: The pope celebrates Mass as he has done almost every day since his ordination in 1946.

Mother Teresa
and
Pope John Paul II
in
India in 1986

Pope John Paul II is a pope unlike any other. No other pope has had his own syndicated newspaper column. No other pope has been able to use satellite television transmissions to spread his message to people throughout the world. Certainly, no other pope has gone directly to the people in the way this Polish pope has. This is a modern man, a man of the jet age, comfortable at center stage, open with his opinions, and straightforward in communicating them. He takes his message to the people.

"When I was a little girl, the pope was almost untouchable," said a Nebraska woman who drove 200 miles to see Pope John Paul when he came to Des Moines in 1979. "Now he's actually walking the earth," she said.

Although Pope Paul VI traveled to the Philippines and India and to the United Nations (in 1965), John Paul II is the first pope to travel the globe. He has been to more than 60 countries, delivering his message of peace, calling all people to love one another, and reminding everyone whose life he touches that, like him, they are called to serve their fellow human beings.

The pope's homilies and addresses are written specifically for the audience at each place he visits, and he does not shy away from rough issues. During his 1979 trip to Ireland, for example, John Paul thundered to a crowd near the border of Northern Ireland: "Thou shall not kill." He called on parents to teach their children reconciliation, not violence.

When he went to Brazil, the pope spoke of the love that the church has for the poor; in Yankee Stadium in New York, he told Americans to give to the poor until it hurts. But there is no greater example of John Paul's sincere wish to communicate with all people, than the visit he made to an Italian prison to meet with the man who tried to end his life.

Pope John Paul had just completed his weekly talk to the crowd gathered in St. Peter's Square on May 13, 1981. As was his custom, he was riding in an open jeep through the thousands of pilgrims and visitors to Rome when Mehmet Ali Agca, a Turkish terrorist, fired several shots with a handgun.

The pope narrowly escaped death. The bullets hit his hand and abdomen, but missed his vital organs. He spent 77 days in a Rome hospital, but by October of 1981, he was again making public appearances.

Above: Aides rushed to assist the pontiff after an assassination attempt on May 13, 1981.

Opposite: John Paul II at an outdoor Mass in France

Two years later, after his attacker had been convicted by an Italian court, Pope John Paul II made a Christmas visit to Agca's prison cell. The moving television footage of his offering of reconciliation was broadcast throughout the world.

If John XXIII had opened the windows, Pope John Paul is opening the doors. Where former popes have worked behind the scenes to influence government policies, this pope confronts government leaders head on. He has met with Andrei Gromyko of the Soviet Union on two occasions.

He has exchanged ambassadors with the British government for the first time since Henry VIII. He has spoken with Yasser Arafat about Middle East peace prospects, faced the politically divergent leaders of Nicaragua and Chile, and denounced anti-Semitism and apartheid.

In 1983, he celebrated the 500th anniversary of the birth of Martin Luther with Protestant church leaders and became the first pope to visit a Lutheran congregation and to join with them in prayer. In 1986, he made an unprecedented visit to Rome's main synagogue and prayed with the oldest Jewish congregation outside of Israel.

Much of Pope John Paul's philosophy can be traced to his upbringing and experiences in Poland, a country where 95 percent of the population is Catholic. The traditions of the church and the celebration of holy days are part of the cultural life of the people. In Poland, thousands walk as pilgrims to shrines like Jasna Gora, the Shrine of Our Lady of Czestochowa. Many carry on the tradition of traveling the last mile on their knees. The piety and fervor of this kind of faith is valued by the pope.

One of his goals, as he travels throughout the world, is to bring unity to humanity. He wants to get people thinking about the spiritual part of their lives. His journeys are intended to help people celebrate their faith and to challenge them to grow in their sense of right and wrong. From Honduras to Hiroshima, from Cameroon to Canada, he calls people to the service of others as a way of serving God. He goes to the people where they are, from the mines of northern Italy to La Scala, the opera house in Milan, from the White House in Washington to a basketball court in Rome. And always John Paul expresses his concern for all people with his teachings about love and justice.

Above: Breaking with tradition, John Paul II visited Rome's main synagogue in 1986.

Opposite: The pope with French and Swiss admirers in Val d'Aosta, 1986

"Bring your families, so that they may continue to be the working, living, and loving community where nature is revered, where burdens are shared, and where the Lord is praised."

"I wish to express my esteem and love for America itself, for the experience that began
two centuries ago and that carries the name 'United States of America';
for the past achievements of this land
and for its dedication to a more just and human future;
for the generosity with which this country has offered shelter, freedom, and a chance
for betterment to all who have come to its shores."

OPPOSITE: WALL STREET   ABOVE: BATTERY PARK

"I have come to carry out a mission entrusted to me by Divine Providence,
the mission of proclaiming the dignity and the fundamental equality of every human being
and his right to live
in a world of justice, peace, brotherhood, and solidarity."

"As one who has always been close to nature, let me speak to you about the land.
The land is God's gift, given by a loving creator
as a means of sustaining the life which he has created. But the land
is not only God's gift.
It is also man's responsibility."

*"The progress of humanity
must be measured not only by the progress of science and technology,
but also by the importance given to spiritual values."*

*"We come from many cultural traditions and religious backgrounds,
but we are united in our common determination
to seek peace and human betterment."*

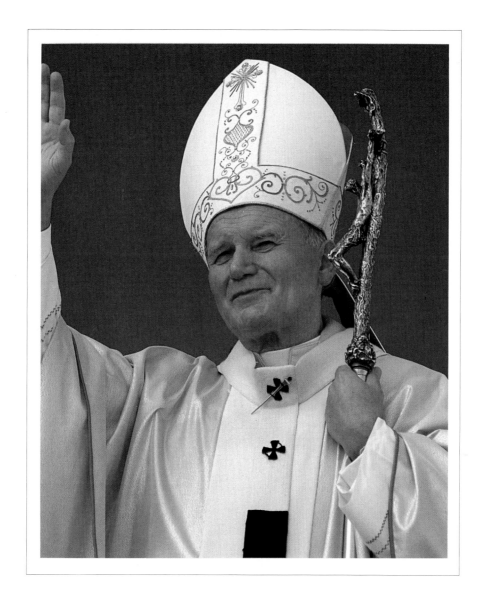

"Cooperation, mutual love, and helping each other make us know one another better and make us rediscover what we have in common."

"Bring with you the poor, the sick, the exiled, and the hungry;
bring all who are weary and find life burdensome.
At this altar they will be refreshed."

*"Make peace the desire of your heart, for if you love peace, you will love
all humanity, without distinction of race, color, or creed."*

"The most important human rights are the right to life, liberty,
and personal safety; the right to freedom of expression;
the right to religion;
the right to found a family and to enjoy all conditions necessary
for family life;
and the right to property and work and a just wage; the right to nationality
and residence; and the right to participate
in the free choice of the government of one's people."

*"Strengthen the bonds that unite us
and eliminate all that has divided us in the past."*

*"The pope wishes to be your voice; the voice of all those who cannot speak,
or who are kept silent; the voice of conscience,
the call to action."*

*"My own spiritual and religious mission impels me to be the messenger of peace
and brotherhood and to witness
to the true greatness of every human person."*

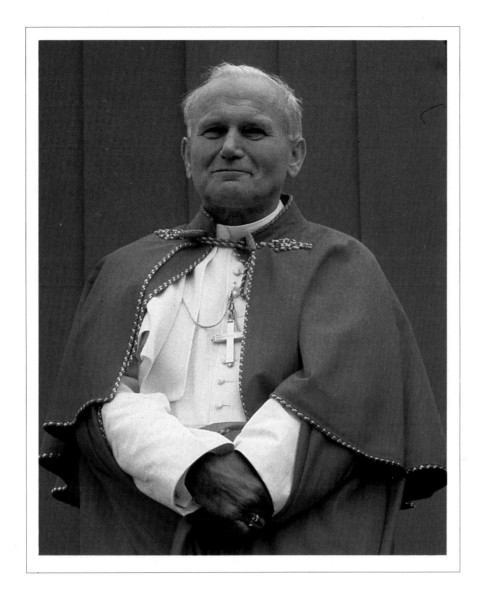

"The absolute and yet gentle power of the Lord
corresponds to the whole depths of the human person, to his loftiest aspirations
of intellect, will, and heart.
It does not speak the language of force, but expresses itself in charity and truth."

OPPOSITE: POPE JOHN PAUL LEAVING MASS IN BOSTON

*"A prudent man is not one who, like so many,
sets out to make life comfortable for himself and to get as much out of it as he can,
but one who measures his life by the yardstick of moral values
and the voice of true conscience."*

"I greet all Americans without distinction.
I want to meet you and tell you all—men and women of all creeds and ethnic origins,
children and youth, fathers and mothers, the sick and the elderly—that God loves you,
that he has given you a dignity
as human beings that is beyond compare.
I want to tell everyone that the pope is your friend and a servant of your humanity."

"We cannot live without love. If we do not encounter love,
if we do not experience it
and make it our own, and if we do not participate intimately in it, our life is meaningless.
Without love we remain incomprehensible to ourselves."

"Do not be afraid
of honest effort and honest work;
do not be afraid of the truth."

ABOVE: BROCCOLI FIELDS NEAR MONTEREY, CALIFORNIA

"What better wish can I express for all the children of the world than a better future in which respect for human rights will become a complete reality."

"The American people bases its concept of life on spiritual and moral values,
on a deep religious sense, on respect for duty, and on generosity in the service of humanity—noble traits
which are embodied in a particular way in the nation's capital, with its monuments dedicated to such outstanding national figures
as George Washington, Abraham Lincoln, and Thomas Jefferson."

"The message of love is always important, always relevant.
It is not difficult to see that despite its beauty and grandeur, despite the conquests of science and technology,
despite the abundant material goods it offers, today's world is yearning for more truth,
for more love, and for more joy."

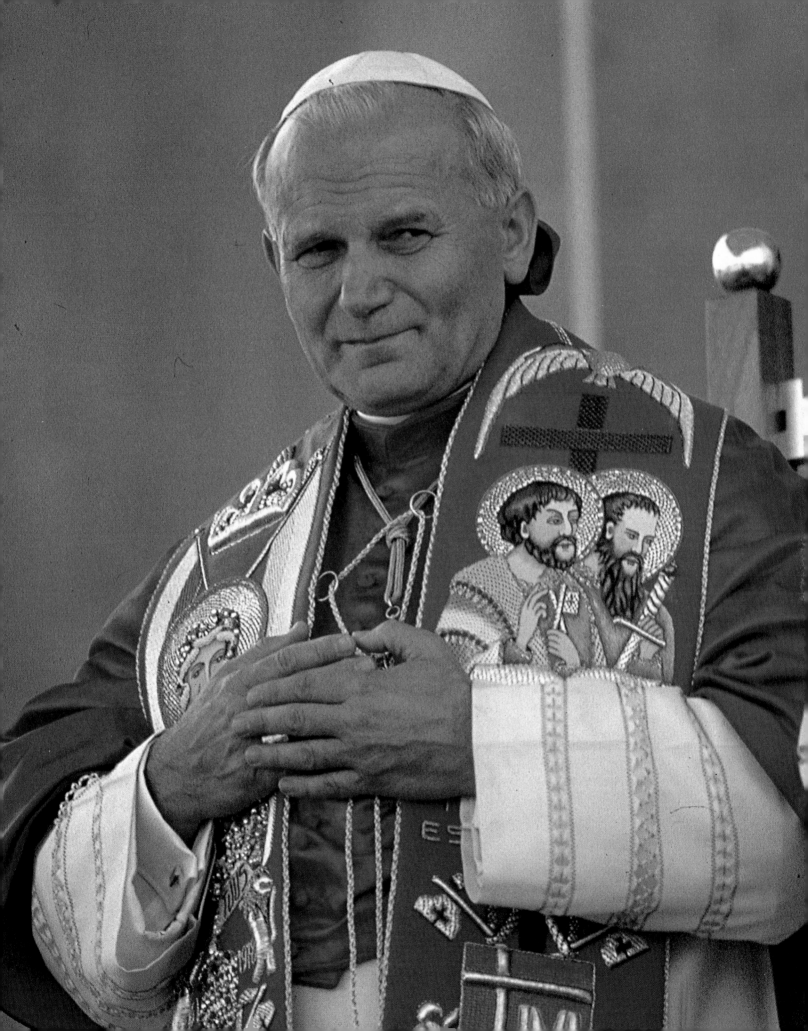

"Every human person, endowed with reason, is free
when he is the master of his own actions,
when he is capable of choosing that good which is in conformity with reason,
and therefore with his own human dignity."

*"Nothing surpasses the greatness or dignity of a human person. Human life
is not just an idea or an abstraction.
Human life is the concrete reality of a being that is capable of love and
of service to humanity."*

*"Human life is precious because it is the gift of a God whose love is infinite;
and when God gives life, it is forever."*

Front Cover Photo: David Burnett/Contact Press Images-Woodfin Camp; Back Cover Photo: Dilip Mehta/Contact Press Images-Woodfin Camp; Inside Photos: Archdiocese of Detroit/Richard Laskos, p. 37; James Blank/Root Resources, p. 58; Edward Bower/The Image Bank, p. 40; David Burnett/Contact Press Images-Woodfin Camp, pp. 1, 21, 24; Tom Dietrich/Click-Chicago, p. 26; Michael Evans/Gamma-Liaison, pp. 22, 38; Fabian/Sygma, p. 14; Chuck Fishman/Contact Press Images-Woodfin Camp, p. 62; Edoardo Fornaciari/Gamma-Liaison, p. 46; Francosimon-Lochon/Gamma-Liaison, p. 59; Gamma-Liaison, pp. 13, 27; Giansanti/Gamma-Liaison, p. 61; Giansanti/Sygma, pp. 10-11, 19, 53, 54, 63; Globe Photos, p. 55; Larry Dale Gordon/The Image Bank, p. 29; Gianfranco Gorgoni/Contact Press Images-Woodfin Camp, pp. 16-17, 23, 49; Chip Hires/Gamma-Liaison, p. 57; J. P. Laffont/Sygma, p. 20; Steve Liss/Gamma-Liaison, p. 44; F. Lochon/Gamma-Liaison, pp. 18, 35, 43, 45, 60, 64; Lochon-Francolon/Gamma-Liaison, pp. 25, 39, 47, 51; Peter Marlow/Sygma, p. 34; A. Nogues/Sygma, p. 15; Michael Norcia/Outline Press, pp. 7, 9, 12, 28, 32, 33, 36, 41; Southern Stock Photos, p. 42; Sygma, p. 4; H. R. Uthoff/The Image Bank, p. 50; Uzan/Gamma-Liaison, pp. 5, 6, 8; Roberto Valladares/The Image Bank, p. 52; Wide World Photos, pp. 48, 56.